D1712926

THE ERUPTION OF MOUNT ST. HELENS

BY THOMAS K. ADAMSON

BELLWETHER MEDIA · MINNEAPOLIS, MN

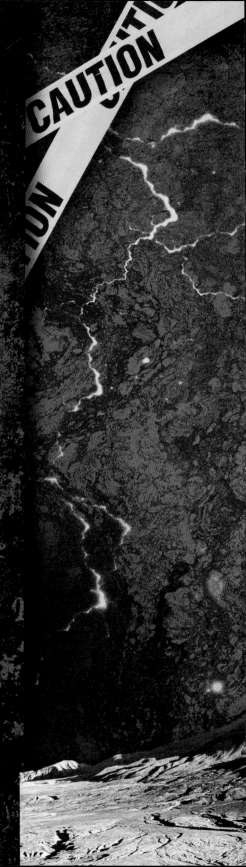

Torque brims with excitement perfect for thrill-seekers of all kinds. Discover daring survival skills, explore uncharted worlds, and marvel at mighty engines and extreme sports. In *Torque* books, anything can happen. Are you ready?

This edition first published in 2022 by Bellwether Media, Inc.

No part of this publication may be reproduced in whole or in part without written permission of the publisher. For information regarding permission, write to Bellwether Media, Inc., Attention: Permissions Department, 6012 Blue Circle Drive, Minnetonka, MN 55343.

Library of Congress Cataloging-in-Publication Data

Names: Adamson, Thomas K., 1970- author.
Title: The eruption of Mount St. Helens / by Thomas K. Adamson.
Description: Minneapolis, MN : Bellwether Media, 2022. | Series: Deadly
    disasters | Includes bibliographical references and index. | Audience:
    Ages 7-12 | Audience: Grades 4-6 | Summary: "Amazing photography
    accompanies engaging information about the eruption of Mount St. Helens.
    The combination of high-interest subject matter and light text is
    intended for students in grades 3 through 7"– Provided by publisher.
Identifiers: LCCN 2021020934 (print) | LCCN 2021020935 (ebook) | ISBN
    9781644875278 (library binding) | ISBN 9781648344350 (ebook)
Subjects: LCSH: Saint Helens, Mount (Wash.)–Eruption, 1980–Juvenile
    literature.
Classification: LCC QE523.S23 A33 2022 (print) | LCC QE523.S23 (ebook) |
    DDC 363.349509797/84–dc23
LC record available at https://lccn.loc.gov/2021020934
LC ebook record available at https://lccn.loc.gov/2021020935

Editor: Kieran Downs   Designer: Josh Brink

Printed in the United States of America, North Mankato, MN.

TABLE OF CONTENTS

MOUNTAIN BLAST ESCAPE

William Dilley looked through his binoculars. In the distance, Mount St. Helens looked strange. The **volcano** was **erupting**!

Gary Rosenquist and Keith Ronnholm began snapping photos. But a cloud of volcanic ash approached fast. The three dashed into a car and sped away. Rocks and mud fell from the sky. Luckily, the three men survived the eruption!

ERUPTION PHOTOS
Gary's photos are the clearest shots of the eruption.

WARNING SIGNS

Mount St. Helens is a volcano in Washington state. The volcano had been quiet since 1857. But on March 16, 1980, many small **earthquakes** rumbled underneath it. The volcano was becoming active.

On March 27, steam exploded from the top of the volcano. Small eruptions continued for weeks.

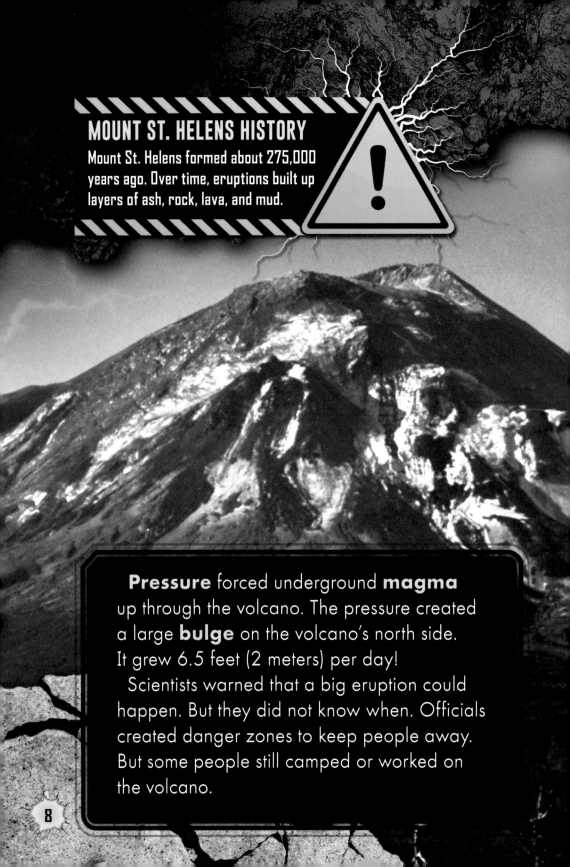

MOUNT ST. HELENS HISTORY

Mount St. Helens formed about 275,000 years ago. Over time, eruptions built up layers of ash, rock, lava, and mud.

Pressure forced underground **magma** up through the volcano. The pressure created a large **bulge** on the volcano's north side. It grew 6.5 feet (2 meters) per day!

Scientists warned that a big eruption could happen. But they did not know when. Officials created danger zones to keep people away. But some people still camped or worked on the volcano.

HOW AN ERUPTION BEGINS

3. THE VOLCANO ERUPTS

MAGMA

2. LANDSLIDE RELEASES PRESSURE

1. PRESSURE FORCES MAGMA UP

VOLCANIC ERUPTION

On May 18, 1980, a strong earthquake shook Mount St. Helens. It caused the largest **landslide** ever recorded. The bulge on the volcano's north side slid down.

The landslide released pressure. This caused the mountain to explode. Hot ash pushed away from the mountain at speeds of up to 300 miles (483 kilometers) per hour.

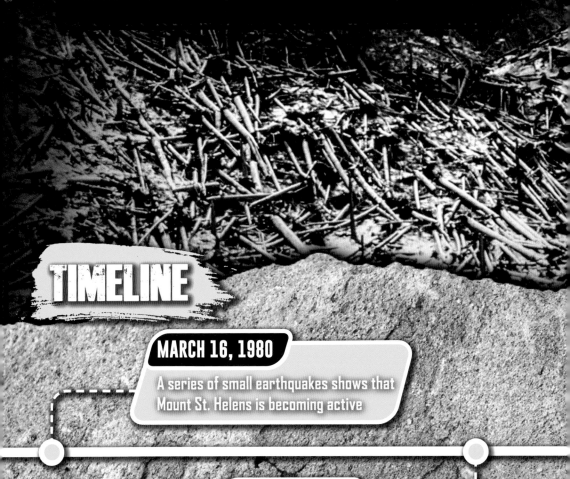

For more than 9 hours, the volcano spewed ash into the sky. It blocked out sunlight, making the day colder.

The cloud of ash spread across the surrounding forest. Its force and speed flattened trees. The blast covered 230 square miles (596 square kilometers) in hot material.

TIMELINE

MARCH 16, 1980

A series of small earthquakes shows that Mount St. Helens is becoming active

MARCH 27, 1980

Mount St. Helens begins erupting for the first time in over 100 years

FLATTENED TREES

MAY 18, 1980, 8:32 A.M.

A large earthquake causes a huge landslide on the north side of the volcano, causing Mount St. Helens to erupt

MAY 18, 1980, 3:00 TO 5:00 P.M.

Mount St. Helens eruption reaches its peak

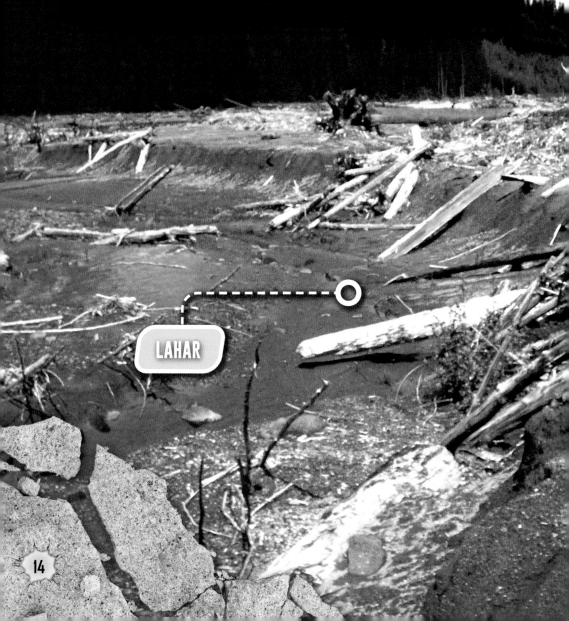

Ash, rock, dirt, and trees swept down the mountain and across the land. Snow and ice on the mountain melted from the heat. The water gushed down the steep slopes. It washed away dirt and rock, creating **lahars**.

These lahars ripped trees out of the ground. They knocked down bridges and destroyed roads.

LAHAR

BLOWN TOP

The eruption took about 1,300 feet (396 meters) off the height of Mount St. Helens. It left a deep crater in the top of the mountain.

MOUNT ST. HELENS CRATER

More than 200 homes were leveled. Many were buried under mud and ash. More than 185 miles (298 kilometers) of roads were wrecked. Millions of trees were destroyed.

Wind carried ash far away from the mountain. The ash had blown around the entire world within two weeks.

ASH

ASH DEPTH

2 TO 5 INCHES (5 TO 13 CENTIMETERS) = ⬭

1/2 TO 2 INCHES (1 TO 5 CENTIMETERS) = ⬭

LESS THAN 1/2 INCH (1 CENTIMETER) = ⬭

BLANKETED IN ASH

Some areas nearly 195 miles (314 kilometers)
away from the blast saw 2 inches
(5 centimeters) of ash fall.

AFTER THE ERUPTION

In the days following the eruption, many cities were covered with ash. This caused breathing problems for many people. Doctors helped make sure cleanup workers had masks to keep them safe. Ash had to be moved off of roads. Trucks hauled ash to dumps. Grass and soil were sometimes piled on top to keep it from blowing around.

CLEANUP WORKERS

NEW GLACIER

After the eruption, a new glacier formed inside the volcano's crater. Named Crater Glacier, it is the newest glacier in the world.

STUDYING AN ACTIVE VOLCANO

Mount St. Helens is still an active volcano. Scientists use **satellite** images and **GPS** to study it. They also study how the landscape is recovering from the eruption.

Mount St. Helens will probably erupt again. Officials study information from the 1980 eruption. They can use it to plan for future eruptions!

PREPARATION KIT

**PLASTIC AND TAPE
TO SEAL OUT ASH**

GOGGLES

MASK

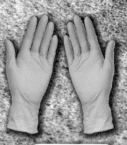

GLOVES

SATELLITE IMAGE OF MOUNT ST. HELENS

bulge—a bump that swells or sticks out

earthquakes—sudden, violent shakings of the earth that may cause damage

erupting—suddenly releasing lava, hot ash, or steam

GPS—global positioning system; GPS is a system of satellites and devices that people use to find locations.

lahars—moving masses of water and volcanic material

landslide—a mass of earth and rocks that suddenly slides down a mountain

magma—melted rock beneath the earth's surface that becomes lava when it flows out of volcanoes

pressure—a force produced by pressing on something

satellite—a spacecraft sent into orbit around Earth; many satellites take pictures of Earth.

volcano—a hole in the earth; when a volcano erupts, hot ash, gas, or melted rock called lava shoots out.

TO LEARN MORE

AT THE LIBRARY

Gomez, Sarah Hannah. *Maribel Versus the Volcano: A Mount St. Helens Survival Story.* North Mankato, Minn.: Stone Arch Books, 2020.

Rose, Simon. *Amazing Volcanoes Around the World.* North Mankato, Minn.: Capstone Press, 2019.

Tarshis, Lauren. *I Survived the Eruption of Mount St. Helens, 1980.* New York, N.Y.: Scholastic Inc., 2016.

ON THE WEB

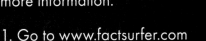

FACTSURFER

Factsurfer.com gives you a safe, fun way to find more information.

1. Go to www.factsurfer.com

2. Enter "Mount St. Helens" into the search box and click 🔍.

3. Select your book cover to see a list of related content.

CAUTION

INDEX

The images in this book are reproduced through the courtesy of: Science History Images/ Alamy Stock Photo, cover, pp. 16-17; 1romm, CIP; Universal Images Group Editorial/ Getty Images, pp. 4-5; Donald A. Swanson/ wikipedia, pp. 6-7; USGS/ Alamy Stock Photo, pp. 8-9; Naeblys, p. 9; World History Archive/ Alamy Stock Photo, pp. 10-11; Everett Collection Inc/ Alamy Stock Photo, pp. 12-13, 14-15; neelsky, p. 15; David R. Frazier Photolibrary, Inc./ Alamy Stock Photo, pp. 18-19; Lyn Topinka/ wikipedia, pp. 20-21; Aleksandr Ryzhov, p. 21 (plastic sheet); Bjoern Wylezich, p. 21 (tape); Oleksandr Kostiuchenko, p. 21 (goggles); Olexandr Panchenko, p. 21 (mask); MariyaL, p. 21 (gloves); Planet Observer/ Alamy Stock Photo, p. 21 (satellite image).